garden project workbooks

beds *and* borders

garden project workbooks

beds *and* borders

Richard Bird

photography by **Stephen Robson**

STEWART, TABORI & CHANG
NEW YORK

First published in 1998 by
Ryland Peters & Small
Cavendish House
51–55 Mortimer Street
London W1N 7TD

Designer **Mark Latter**
Design Assistants **Veronica Wood, Liz Brown**
Editors **Sarah Polden, Sydne Matus**
Production **Kate Mackillop**

Published in 1998 by
Stewart, Tabori & Chang,
a division of U.S. Media Holdings, Inc.
115 West 18th Street, New York, NY 10011

Distributed in Canada by
General Publishing Company Ltd.
30 Lesmill Road
Don Mills, Ontario, Canada M3B 2T6

Library of Congress Cataloging-in-Publication Data

Bird, Richard.
    Beds and borders/Richard Bird; photography by
Stephen Robson.
        p. cm. – (Garden project workbook)
    ISBN 1–55670–689–8
    1. Beds (Gardens) 2. Garden borders.
3. Plants, Ornamental. I. Title. II. Series.
SB423.7.B56   1998
635.9'62–dc21   97–35548
                                  CIP

Printed in China
10 9 8 7 6 5 4 3 2 1

contents

The use of borders is the very essence of gardening.
They are a means of producing a pleasant environment that
is a joy to be in. They can excite or soothe depending on the
mood created. They can be filled with color or present a
mantle of foliage. Beds and borders can appeal to all the
senses: the sense of smell, of course, and sound—why not plant
a bed especially to enjoy the soothing rustle of leaves, grasses
and bamboos, easing the mind—and even taste, as many
flowers are edible. Borders are the backdrop against which you
can relax and enjoy the pleasures of an outside space.

The projects in this book cover a broad range of borders that
can be created using a wide variety of plants. Most can be
modified for any size garden, from a small courtyard to a
number of acres. Adaptability is the key. While you are free
to copy faithfully what is described, you are encouraged to
experiment and extend your own experience. Add or
substitute plants that you like or whose colors you prefer.
Use this book as a jumping-off point, and with patience your
efforts will be amply rewarded.

Richard Bird

above Formality is not always wanted. Here, cottage-style charm is given by *Allium schoenoprasum*, or chives.

above Mixed borders allow a pleasing variety of shapes and forms: scabiosa and salvias mingle with roses.

above Always consider how flower forms will combine as well as colors. A cluster of star shapes looks cheerful.

traditional borders take many forms

and can be adapted at will to suit any garden. Annuals bring a flash of strong color or subtler hue and are ideal for graphic planting schemes, single colors bring harmony, and the classic herbaceous border cannot be matched for the impression of abundance and variety it lends to a garden. Borders and beds are important focal points so they should be created with care.

above A well-conceived border will give color, height, variety, and a clear mood to a garden. It will add inspiring forefront focus or clear background interest to a view.

left Fill upright spaces so that the eye is led through the scheme, as here. Low-growing edging plants are linked by the midheight lilies to a prominent honeysuckle-clad rose. The space is well filled without appearing congested or confused.

above Foliage is there to be
enjoyed in its own right as
well as to make a fine foil
to bold blooms. It affords
a wealth of different shapes,
textures, and colors, as well
as the permanence of
evergreen displays.

right A harmonious color
scheme in a border can be
enhanced by using a similar
palette beyond the border.
Here, verbascum is coupled
with the fine champagne
rose, Graham Thomas, and
Rosa 'Frau Karl Druschki.'

left Plants have a way of softening edges and
blending. Fanning phlox, foxgloves, and
alliums weave toward dark aquilegias.

below Movement and rhythm are at the heart
of this interesting foliage scheme, which is
punctuated by subtle flower tones.

herbaceous border

HERBACEOUS BORDERS ARE BACK! Having suffered a decline in the earlier part of the twentieth century, interest in herbaceous plants has never been so great. They are versatile, presenting the gardener with a tremendous range of colors, shapes, textures, and scents, and despite a reputation for being labor-intensive, they take less looking after than many shrubs such as roses. For those who have been wary of using herbaceous plants, a whole new world is there to be explored.

Planting Scheme

1 *Achillea millefolium* 'Cerise Queen' (× 5)
2 *Achillea filipendulina* 'Gold Plate' (× 6)
3 *Alchemilla mollis* (× 3)
4 *Aquilegia* 'Crimson Star' (× 9)
5 *Asphodeline lutea* (× 5)
6 *Astilbe chinensis* var. *pumila* (× 3)
7 *Eremurus* subsp. *stenophyllus* (× 1)
8 *Euphorbia griffithii* 'Fireglow' (× 3)
9 *Helenium autumnale* (× 3)

10 *Helianthus* 'Loddon Gold' (× 1)
11 *Hemerocallis* 'Marion Vaughn' (× 1)
12 *Kniphofia* 'Percy's Pride' (× 1)
13 *Lychnis chalcedonica* (× 3)
14 *Malva moschata* (× 3)
15 *Mimulus* 'Royal Velvet' (× 3)
16 *Nectaroscordum siculum* (× 12)
17 *Oenothera fruticosa* 'Fyreverken' (× 2)

18 *Oenothera stricta* (× 2)
19 *Penstemon* 'Andenken an Friedrich Hahn' (× 1)
20 *Polemonium pauciflorum* (× 4)
21 *Sedum* 'Ruby Glow' (× 2)
22 *Solidago cutleri* (× 1)
23 *Solidago* 'Laurin' (× 1)
24 *Trifolium rubens* (× 1)
25 *Verbascum bombyciferum* (× 3)

Spring underplanting

Herbaceous borders usually come into their own from early summer onward. Because of the dense growth required to keep a plant in flower right through to autumn, it is difficult to accommodate spring flowers as well. However, there are a few, bulbs in particular, that can be used as they soon die back and take up little or no space later in the year. Winter-flowering pansies and forget-me-nots can be taken out as the herbaceous growth begins.

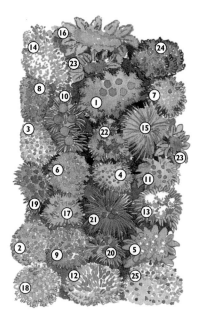

Alternative Planting

1 *Delphinium* hybrids (× 6)
2 *Campanula portenschlagiana* (× 3)
3 *Veronica* 'Shirley Blue' (× 3)
4 *Veronica longifolia* (× 3)
5 *Eryngium alpinum* (× 3)
6 *Geranium* 'Johnson's Blue' (× 1)
7 *Salvia uliginosa* (× 3)
8 *Salvia × sylvestris* 'Blauhügel' (× 1)
9 *Aster × frikartii* 'Mönch' (× 1)

10 *Agapanthus* 'Bressingham Blue' (× 3)
11 *Echinops ritro* (× 1)
12 *Perovskia atriplicifolia* (× 1)
13 *Campanula lactiflora* (× 1)
14 *Aster ericoides* 'Blue Star' (× 1)
15 *Miscanthus sinensis* (× 1)
16 *Salvia sclarea* var. *turkestanica* (× 3)
17 *Bupleurum falcatum* (× 3)

18 *Argyranthemum* 'Jamaica Primrose' (× 3)
19 *Antirrhinum* 'Yellow Triumph' (× 5)
20 *Lilium* 'Limelight' (× 3)
21 *Kniphofia* 'Yellow Hammer' (× 1)
22 *Oenothera stricta* (× 3)
23 *Verbascum bombyciferum* (× 5)
24 *Baptisia australis* (× 1)
25 *Nigella damascena* (× 5)

Selecting colors

Because herbaceous plants are so diverse, the palette of a bed can be controlled very successfully. This alternative scheme is "cool" where the main scheme is "hot."

THE SECRET OF CREATING a successful herbaceous border is to make certain that the ground is prepared thoroughly before planting begins. It is essential that all perennial weeds are removed and generous quantities of well-rotted organic matter are added because the border will not be dug again for several years. Such preparations are well worth the time and effort involved.

Designing

There is no definitive shape for a herbaceous border; it should be designed to fit the space available. However, if possible, the bed should be wide; the ideal is a width of at least twice the height of the tallest plants to be used. This border is 12 × 20 ft (3.5 × 6 m). A backdrop of a green hedge will help to display the flowers to advantage, although an island bed makes a fine focal point. The border should have the tallest flowers at the back and shorter ones toward the front. Plan the arrangement of plants on paper before planting and cater for year-round interest by including plants for each season.

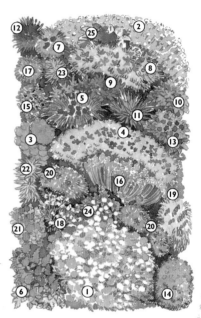

Spacing

If you want to create an abundant look quickly, arrange the plants in close proximity. If you can wait, which is better, allow more growing room.

Care and Maintenance
- *In autumn, tidy the border, removing dead and dying growth; follow with a mulch.*
- *Make sure the bed does not become too congested because this can harm and even kill plants.*
- *Divide vigorous plants regularly, discarding the older sections.*

11

single-color bed

NOTHING IMPRESSES VISITORS to a garden as much as a border devoted to one color. The white garden at Sissinghurst and the red one at Hidcote, two of the finest English gardens, are famous throughout the world and have been much copied. Even when inspiration is taken from an exemplary planting, individual gardeners can make their own choice and arrangement of plants, creating a single-color border very much their own.

Planting Scheme

Perennials
1 *Alcea rugosa* (× 3)
2 *Anemone hupehensis* var. *japonica* 'Prinz Heinrich' (× 3)
3 *Aster novi-belgii* 'Carnival' (× 3)
4 *Aster novae-angliae* 'Andenken an Alma Pötschke' (× 3)
5 *Astilbe × arendsii* 'Fanal' (× 3)
6 *Centranthus ruber* (× 3)
7 *Echinacea purpurea* (× 3)
8 *Filipendula rubra* (× 5)
9 *Geranium psilostemon* (× 1)

10 *Geranium* 'Ann Folkard' (× 1)
11 *Lupinus* 'The Chatelaine' (× 1)
12 *Lychnis viscaria* 'Flore Pleno' (× 3)
13 *Lythrum virgatum* 'The Rocket' (× 2)
14 *Penstemon* 'Evelyn' (× 1)
15 *Penstemon* 'Andenken an Friedrich Hahn' (× 1)
16 *Persicaria affinis* (× 3)
17 *Physostegia virginiana* 'Red Beauty' (× 3)

18 *Sanguisorba obtusa* (× 3)
19 *Sedum telephium* subsp. *maximum* 'Atropurpureum' (× 3)
20 *Sedum spectabile* (× 3)

Bulbs
21 *Crinum × powellii* (× 3)
22 *Dahlia* 'Betty Bowen' (× 3)
23 *Schizostylis coccinea* (× 5)
24 *Tulipa* 'Queen of Night' (× 7)

Shrubs
25 *Deutzia × elegantissima* (× 1)
26 *Rosa* 'Mme. Isaac Pereire' (× 1)

Annuals
27 *Antirrhinum majus* 'His Excellency' (× 7)
28 *Atriplex hortensis* var. *rubra* (× 5)
29 *Dianthus chinensis* 'Firecarpet' (× 5)
30 *Papaver somniferum* (× 3)
31 *Verbena* 'Showtime' (× 7)

Alternative scheme: a white border

The classic single-color border is white, which produces a timeless, restful effect. Pure whites and creamy whites do not combine well, so select plants with care.

Alternative Planting

Perennials
1 *Achillea ptarmica* The Pearl Group (× 3)
2 *Digitalis purpurea* 'Alba' (× 3)
3 *Anemone × hybrida* 'Honorine Jobert' (× 3)
4 *Gypsophila paniculata* 'Bristol Fairy' (× 1)
5 *Polygonatum × hybridum* (× 1)
6 *Phlox paniculata* 'Fujiyama' (× 1)
7 *Lamium maculatum* 'White Nancy' (× 3)
8 *Dianthus* 'Haytor White' (× 3)
9 *Anaphalis margaritacea* (× 1)
10 *Stachys byzantina* (× 3)
11 *Smilacina racemosa* (× 1)
12 *Epilobium angustifolium* 'Album' (× 2)
13 *Pulmonaria officinalis* 'Sissinghurst White' (× 3)

Bulbs
14 *Tulipa* 'Maureen' (× 6)
15 *Cosmos* 'Purity' (× 4)

Shrubs
16 *Rosa* Iceberg (× 1)
17 *Exochorda × macrantha* 'The Bride' (× 1)
18 *Artemisia* 'Powis Castle' (× 1)
19 *Clematis* 'Marie Boisselot' (× 1)

Annuals
20 *Omphalodes linifolia* (× 5)
21 *Nicotiana sylvestris* (× 3)
22 *Antirrhinum* 'White Wonder' (× 5)

Seasonal interest

The essential factor to remember for all borders is seasonal interest. A border or bed is not truly successful if its period of interest is limited to a glorious midsummer display, with nothing of significance in spring, late summer, or autumn. With single-color beds the challenge is all the greater to find early- and late-flowering plants that take up the color idea. This consistency is important because seasons of interest overlap.

ALTHOUGH IT MAY seem a simple goal, creating a border from a single color is not easy. There are many different shades of any one color and they do not always combine well. Yellow, for example, has two distinct forms, orange-yellows and green-yellows. Similarly, blue-reds and orange-reds are quite different in character and do not mix. There are no fixed rules for evaluating a plant's color and it is really a question of developing an eye for blending tones.

The foliage factor
Most green leaves complement a wide range of flower colors. Variegated plants, however, should be used with caution: a strident golden variegation in the middle of this romantic pink corner bed, 12 × 12 ft (3.5 × 3.5 m), would spoil the effect completely. Similarly, silver and purple foliage can strike a jarring note unless they take up the theme of your color scheme, so always look beyond the shade of the flower to the foliage effect to avoid disappointment. To be true to your scheme, remove any mismatched plants.

Secondary colors
Introducing a second color into what is predominantly a single-colored border can be most effective. The second color might serve to create a focal point or to relieve what has become a dull scene. The overall color scheme is retained but made more interesting.

bedding border

AMONG THE MOST COLORFUL elements of Victorian gardens were bedding borders. Some schemes were simple, just blocks of colors, while others were complicated designs that involved thousands of plants. By using a propagating frame or greenhouse it is possible to produce all the plants required for a bedding display at low cost, and the rewards are great for the effort needed. Especially efffective as front gardens, these borders will make their mark in any formal design.

Planting Scheme

1 *Cordyline australis* (× 1)
2 *Echeveria pulvinata* (× 8 per yd/per m)
3 *Echeveria secunda* var. *glauca* (× 8 per yd/per m)
4 *Sedum acre* (× 150 per sq yd/per sq m)
5 *Echeveria elegans* (× 10 per yd/per m)
6 *Alternanthera* 'Aurea Nana' (× 150 per sq yd/per sq m)
7 *Alternanthera* 'Brilliantissima' (× 150 per sq yd/per sq m)
8 *Alternanthera* 'Versicolor' (× 150 per sq yd/per sq m)
9 *Dudleya farinosa* (× 12 per yd/per m)

A modern touch
Bedding displays are often viewed as old-fashioned, but the wealth of plants available today and the preference for clear-cut graphic planting make bedding ideal. A group of small beds will enliven the smallest city courtyard. Look for inspiration beyond the garden, in books on tapestry, cross-stitch, or quilting (below and right).

Square Bed
1 *Tagetes* Bonanza Series
  (× 36 per sq yd/per sq m)
2 *Tagetes* 'Vanilla'
  (× 25 per sq yd/per sq m)

Diamond Bed
1 *Viola cornuta* 'Victoria
  Cawthorne'
  (× 25 per sq yd/per sq m)
2 *Viola* 'Ardross Gem'
  (× 25 per sq yd/per sq m)
3 *Viola pedata*
  (× 25 per sq yd/per sq m)
4 *Viola* 'Huntercombe Purple'
  (× 25 per sq yd/per sq m)

THE REAL SKILL WITH BEDDING DISPLAYS is devising the design. Simple shapes can be very effective and bold; by contrast, a complicated design will sit very well in a knot garden. A personal emblem or figurative elements such as butterflies and birds can be incorporated into a design. Bedding plants are short-lived, so there is room for experimentation.

Plants

Annuals are not the only kind of bedding plants; there are countless others that work just as well, including perennials, succulents, and houseplants. Think of the colors and textures you require, then look for the best candidates.

Planning a bedding scheme

If the design is complicated, work it out to scale on graph paper to get the proportions right and to calculate how many plants will be needed. This scheme is 10 × 20 ft (3 × 6 m) but it can be adapted to the size of your garden.

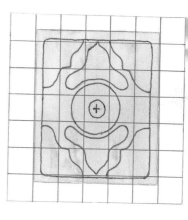

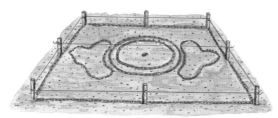

Marking out the scheme

Prepare the soil, then mark out the design on the surface using light-colored sand. The grid from your paper plan can be transferred using strings or lengths of wood.

Planting the bed

Assemble all your plants, making sure you have enough to complete the job. Starting from the middle of the bed or border and working out to the edges, plant the design. Use a plank if necessary as a bridge from which to work. Trim and neaten the plants as you go because you may not be able to reach the center again.

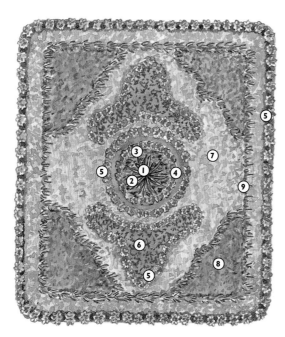

Care and Maintenance
- *Tender plants, as here, should not be planted until the threat of frost is well past.*
- *Keep the bed weed free.*
- *Preserve or propagate plants for use the following year.*

foliage bed

FOLIAGE HAS A GREAT advantage over flowers: It is present for most of
the growing season or, in the case of evergreens, throughout the year.
A foliage garden or border need never be boring. It can be a very cool,
restful place, especially if the colors, shapes, and textures have been
grouped in a sympathetic manner. By contrast and for a flamboyant
touch, there are exotic and brightly colored foliage plants to
create a party atmosphere and huge-leaved plants to add drama.

Planting Scheme

1 *Phytolacca americana*
(× 1)

2 *Cornus controversa*
'Variegata' (× 1)

3 *Geranium
macrorrhizum* (× 7)

4 *Polystichum setiferum*
(× 1)

5 *Geranium palmatum*
(× 3)

6 *Geranium ×
magnificum* (× 3)

7 *Iris sibirica*
(× 3)

8 *Lysimachia ciliata*
'Firecracker'
(× 1)

9 *Meconopsis cambrica*
(× 6)

10 *Euphorbia characias*
subsp. *wulfenii* (× 3)

11 *Macleaya cordata*
(× 3)

12 *Romneya coulteri*
(× 2)

13 *Lysichiton
americanus* (× 1)

14 *Kniphofia* 'Painted
Lady' (× 1)

15 *Crocosmia ×
crocosmiiflora*
'Solfaterre' (× 3)

16 *Hosta lancifolia*
(× 1)

17 *Heuchera micrantha*
var. *diversifolia* 'Palace
Purple' (× 3)

18 *Hosta* Tardiana
Group 'Halcyon' (× 3)

19 *Euphorbia dulcis*
'Chameleon'
(× 1)

20 *Miscanthus sinensis*
(× 1)

21 *Ferula communis*
(× 1)

22 *Rodgersia podophylla*
(× 1)

23 *Silybum marianum*
(× 3)

Alternative scheme: silver and blue bed

There are many colors beyond shades of green that can be used in a foliage scheme, and one of the most restful is silver. Many silver and gray plants have soft foliage and a loose, spreading growing pattern that are ideal for an asymmetrical scheme but also work very well in a more formal planting, as in this example.

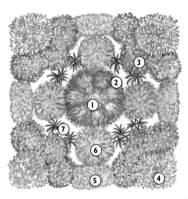

Combining colors

In this design, pale blue and light pink flowers complement the silver foliage, lifting the overall impression made by the bed without detracting from the delicacy of the foliage shades.

Alternative Planting

1 *Pyrus salicifolia* 'Pendula' (× 1)
2 *Artemisia* 'Powis Castle' (× 7)
3 *Nepeta × faassenii* (× 12)
4 *Stachys byzantina* (× 12)
5 *Dianthus* 'Inchmery' (× 12)
6 *Veronica spicata* subsp. *incana* (× 4)
7 *Nerine bowdenii* (× 16)

Other colored foliage

Silver is one of the few colors other than green that will sustain an entire foliage scheme. Purple foliage is very bold when it punctuates a green planting but dull if massed, as are gold and bronze. Variegated plants can add confusion if used without restraint. However, all are excellent as foliage highlights.

Care and Maintenance

• *Remove any spent flowering stems, leaving the foliage to provide the interest. The foliage of* Geranium magnificum *should be cut after flowering to encourage a fresh crop of leaves.*
• *In autumn remove any dead foliage and top-dress with organic matter. Tie up the kniphofia foliage in a bunch above the crown to protect it.*
• *In spring remove any remaining old foliage including that of the ferns and the kniphofia.*

SINCE ALL PLANTS HAVE leaves in one form or another, there are no limits
to the mood and effect that can be created using foliage. Some plants, such as
hostas and grasses, are used primarily as foliage plants; for the wealth of plants
where flowers are prominent, blooms must be an asset to the green scheme.

Foliage forms

When choosing plants, look at the shapes of the leaves as well as their color. A mixture
of shapes is usually much more interesting than a multiplication of a single leaf form,
although other qualities in the leaf—fleshy or fine, shiny or matte—should also be
considered for a well blended planting as in this square bed, 18 × 18 ft (5.5 × 5.5 m).

mixed border

THE USE OF MIXED PLANTINGS has become the favorite form of ornamental gardening. Shrubs combined with perennials give a bed a sense of permanence and structure that lasts throughout the year, even during the winter months. Spring bulbs provide drifts of color and annuals make valuable contributions—they can be changed each year, thereby altering the general appearance of the border, they quickly fill gaps, and their bright colors add a touch of gaiety.

Planting Scheme

1 *Primula* 'Blue Riband'
   (× 5)
2 *Papaver somniferum*
   (× 4)
3 *Rosa gallica* var. *officinalis*
   'Versicolor' (× 1)
4 *Aruncus dioicus* (× 1)
5 *Pyrus salicifolia*
   'Pendula'(× 1)
6 *Delphinium* 'Fenella'
   (× 2)

7 *Salvia forsskaolii* (× 3)
8 *Veronica* 'Shirley Blue'
   (× 2)
9 *Geranium* × *riversleaianum*
   'Mavis Simpson' (× 1)
10 *Leymus arenarius* (× 1)
11 *Dianthus* 'Doris' (× 3)
12 *Sisyrinchium striatum*
   (× 4)
13 *Baptisia australis* (× 1)

14 *Salvia forsskaolii* (× 3)
15 *Trifolium rubens* (× 1)
16 *Papaver orientale*
   'Mrs Perry' (× 1)
17 *Silene dioica* (× 2)
18 *Lilium regale* (× 3)
19 *Campanula persicifolia*
   (× 1)
20 *Salvia sclarea* (× 1)
21 *Tanacetum vulgare* (× 5)
22 *Viola cornuta* (× 3)

Pruning

The *Rosa glauca* in this border can be pruned heavily each spring, removing the old wood almost to the ground. This looks drastic but will encourage new shoots with masses of richly colored foliage.

Spring planting

To provide interest in early spring, plant daffodils and dark-colored tulips between the existing planting. The emerging herbaceous foliage will cover the bulbs' dying leaves which can also be cut off once they begin to turn brown.

Other partners for yellow

Yellow is one of the most versatile colors in the garden. It represents a huge section of garden plants and works very well with other colors, in different ways.

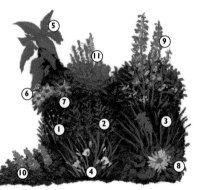

Yellow and Blue

1 *Anthemis tinctoria*
2 *Helianthus* 'Lemon Queen'
3 *Kniphofia* Yellow Hammer'
4 *Oenothera stricta*
5 *Verbascum olympicum*
6 *Aquilegia flabellata*
7 *Eryngium × tripartitum*
8 *Aster × frikartii*
9 *Delphinium* hybrids
10 *Veronica* 'Shirley Blue'
11 *Veronica longifolia*

Yellow and Orange

1 *Anthemis tinctoria*
2 *Helianthus* 'Lemon Queen'
3 *Kniphofia* Yellow Hammer'
4 *Oenothera stricta*
5 *Verbascum olympicum*
6 *Canna* 'Orange Perfection'
7 *Crocosmia × crocosmiiflora*
 'Emily McKenzie'
8 *Dahlia* 'Bishop of Llandaff'
9 *Euphorbia griffithii* 'Fireglow'
10 *Geum* 'Borisii'
11 *Papaver atlanticum*

FOR A TWO-COLOR BORDER, choose the plants carefully. It may be best to plan the border over several seasons, carrying a notebook to jot down suitable plants as you see them in other gardens. Shrubs, perennials, annuals, and grasses can all be used to good effect; take cuttings or divide plants to ensure that the color will remain consistent. This 6 × 15 ft (1.8× 4.5 m) border has year-round interest.

Selecting colors

Choosing colors is a personal matter; we all have our favorites and dislikes. But before two colors are selected, certain factors should be considered. Does the combination work or jar—there are certainly many pairings that are not as successful as others, such as red and white or orange and purple. Can the shades of the chosen plants be restricted effectively? For example, using every tone of pink could be busy enough without adding another color. And does the combination create the desired mood?

Care and Maintenance

• *Cut the lupins back to the ground when they have finished flowering or just remove the old flower spikes to encourage a second crop of smaller flowers.*
• *Cut the* Anthemis *to the ground after flowering to encourage fresh foliage.*
• *Allow the self-sowing annuals and biennials limited time to seed to prevent overcrowding. Thin the resulting seedlings as they emerge.*
• *Cut back dead foliage in autumn.*
• *Tie the kniphofia leaves in a bunch over the crown of the plant for winter protection and then cut the leaves away in spring as the new foliage emerges.*
• *Top-dress in the winter with well-rotted organic material.*

above The shapes of beds are better defined if they are outlined by a low hedge which prevents the plants flopping over the edge.

above A combination of paths and hedges weave a tapestry in this cottage garden. The low, contained planting enhances the shapes.

shaped borders are rewarding to create;

almost any shape can be used, whether geometric or free-flowing, although sharp points are difficult to plant unless they have first been lined with a low hedge. Circular beds have elegance, a sinuous border charm; a parterre is the ultimate expression of order and complexity.

above Curved, meandering lines to a border are much more interesting than a straight edge, especially when the planting is informal, as here.

above right A simple or symmetrical design featuring a central plant or ornament uses a circular bed to best advantage.

right A clean edge between a planted border and an area of grass always helps to enhance the shape of the border.

above Large patterned areas can be most effective, especially if they can be viewed from above, as from the raised walkway over this delightful well-planned parterre.

left The use of shaped borders is a good approach to designing single-colored gardens. Here, the shapes fit perfectly into the available space and set off the pattern of the brick path.

below A circular rose bed surrounded by a gravel path —a picturesque corner of a fine garden. Small hedges extend into the circle, leading the eye toward the birdbath in the middle, an imaginative, witty device.

round bed

To MANY PEOPLE the words "border" and "bed" conjure up the image of a long strip of cultivated ground, but in fact there is no reason why a planted space should not be any shape. One of the most popular is a round bed, situated in the middle of a lawn or surrounded by a path. The symmetry of a circle is particularly effective in a formal garden; a classical approach is a group of four circular beds. By contrast, filled with annuals, the bed becomes a very cheerful, informal feature.

Planting Scheme

1 *Allium cristophii* (× 1)
2 *Artemisia alba* 'Canescens' (× 10)
3 *Milium effusum* (× 5)
4 *Rosa* 'Ballerina' (× 5)
5 *Scabiosa caucasica* 'Clive Greaves' (× 5)
6 *Viola,* mixed pink and blue (numerous)

Alternative scheme: a wheel

One of the most effective ways to plant a round bed is to create a spoked wheel, with a central pivot, radiating bands, and planted "spaces," and an edging, each containing a single variety of plant. Use color wisely, with a restricted palette of complementary tones.

Alternative Planting

1 *Stachys byzantina* (× 4)
2 *Salvia patens* (× 60)
3 *Salvia fulgens* (× 60)
4 *Heliotropium arborescens*
   'P. K. Lowther' (× 60)

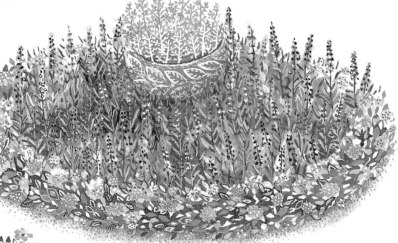

Care and Maintenance

• *With closely planted beds such as these, it is important to keep plant growth neat, otherwise the bed can look crowded and unkempt.*
• *Tread carefully to cause minimal disturbance when pruning a standard rose or topiary centerpiece.*

THERE ARE SEVERAL ways of planting a round bed, depending on its role in the garden. In an informal setting, a border of mixed plants, randomly planted, can look very effective. For a formal design, order is the essential element, often with a central axis: a standard rose, planted urn, or piece of statuary.

Creating the circle

There is a simple method for marking out a circular bed. Place a stake or strong stick where the center is to be. Tie a length of string to this and at the desired diameter tie another stick. Keeping the string taut, walk around, scoring a circle in the ground.

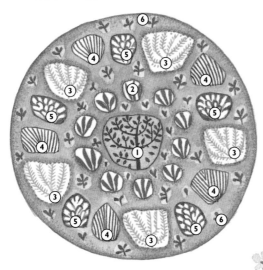

Creating an oval

Another pleasing bed shape is an oval. This is easily marked out by outlining two circles (as above) and joining them with straight lines. When planning the length of such a bed, remember that the radius of the circles is an important measurement. Use a tall plant at the center of each "circle."

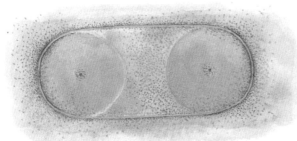

Planting

As with all symmetrical schemes, the rule is to start at the centre and work outwards. Plan the bed on paper first; even a small bed can take a lot of undoing if things go wrong. This example measures 10 ft (3 m) across.

Ideas for round beds

The simplest solution, well suited to a formal garden, is a bed devoted almost entirely to one variety of plant, perhaps with a single tree or bush in the center and a low box hedge or edging around the perimeter. Alternatively, for a more contemporary look, a bold pattern can be created using bedding plants: a jagged gash of color across the bed or a series of concentric circles.

parterre

ALTHOUGH PARTERRES may seem appropriate only to stately homes, many a small town garden contains one, scaled down and designed to enhance the size and shape available. In essence, a parterre is a formal arrangement of beds to create a geometric or more fluid pattern. Typically, the edges are delineated by low hedges or brickwork, with the enclosed spaces filled with plants of contrasting colors. The results are pleasing to the eye and at their best provide year-round interest.

Planting Scheme

1 *Buxus sempervirens* 'Suffruticosa' (9 per yd/per m)
2 *Sedum* 'Herbstfreude'
(4 per sq yd/per sq m)
3 *Begonia* × *carrierei* 'Red Ascot'
(36 per sq yd/per sq m)
4 *Nicotiana langsdorffii* (9 per sq yd/per sq m)
5 *Verbena* 'Blue Lagoon'
(9 per sq yd/per sq m)

Brick parterre

In marked, and some might say refreshing, contrast to traditional planted parterres are brick-based designs. These are ideal for smaller city gardens and are the answer for anyone seeking the order and impact of a parterre without waiting years to see hedging at its best. Much of the interest lies in the pattern of the brickwork but by no means all. The same principle applies as for planted parterres when filling beds. Use blocks of color or single plants. If space is limited, a clever and witty approach is to fill the compartments with vegetables and herbs. In this way, a modern courtyard can become a traditional herb garden.

Alternative Planting

onions	9 cabbages
Swiss chard	10 red lettuce
lettuce	11 bok choy
chives	12 zucchini
leeks	13 radishes
parsley	14 climbing beans
Brussels sprouts	15 carrots
beets	

Shapes

Parterres have taken all manner of shapes over the centuries. Favorite devices are trompe l'oeil effects, with "overlapping" beds and dynamic curlicues. All were conceived in the name of elegance, formality, style, and wit.

42

THERE IS NO RIGHT or wrong way to create a parterre. A designer's imagination can run free, making the pattern as simple or as complicated as he or she wants. Although curves soften a design, an entirely straight-edged parterre can be very successful. Much of the overall impact of a parterre lies in the viewing and it will always be more impressive if viewed from above, from a terrace or window.

A formal parterre

Much of the challenge in producing a beautiful traditional parterre lies in the plant selection. Starting with the framework, the best growing border is dwarf box, but other good candidates include lavender—with the bonus of its fragrance—santolina, and teucrium. Traditionally, each bed should be made up of plants of a single color or sometimes two colors. Annuals allow for and demand a yearly change; small shrubs form a permanent planting. High on the list should come antirrhinums, begonias, diascias, lobelias, impatiens, salvias, and violas. Parterres do not have to be large. This fine one is 15 × 20 ft (4.5 × 6 m).

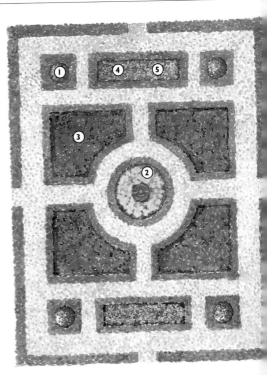

Care and Maintenance
- *Keep the box hedging well trimmed*
- *Keep gravel paths well raked.*
- *Do not make the contained beds too large, otherwise planting and trimming will be very difficult.*

41

corner planting

ALL GARDENS HAVE ODD CORNERS, and since most gardeners
complain that they never have enough space, it makes sense to use all
these pockets. Another advantage of filling these corners is that it helps
to unify the garden, to create an overall picture. A common solution
is to use bland ground cover plants to fill such areas, but it is far better
to think ideas through and create something interesting like this
simple, cool-looking border. Make every inch count.

Planting Scheme

1 *Alchemilla alpina* (× 9)
2 *Euphorbia stricta* (× 4)
3 *Mimulus guttatus* (× 3)
4 *Deschampsia flexuosa* (× 2)
5 *Geranium pratense* 'Mrs Kendall Clark' (× 1)
6 *Alchemilla conjuncta* (× 1)

corner planting

Alternative scheme: a small rock garden

A well-constructed, well-planted rock garden is an excellent solution for many corners. The rule is to bury at least half of each rock in the soil—this will secure it and provide a cool, moist root-run. Arrange rocks in tiers, all leaning back slightly.

Safety considerations

Never lift more than you can comfortably handle and protect your fingers from crushing stones. Get help if necessary. Move large rocks using a strong pole as a lever or roll rather than lift them. Make sure all rocks are secure.

Designing a rock garden

Rock gardens are intended to replicate rocky outcrops, so aim for strata of rocks that are similar in size but not too orderly.

Alternative Planting

Daphne tangutica (× 1)
Juniperus communis 'Compressa' (× 1)
Picea mariana 'Nana' (× 1)
Helianthemum 'Annabel' (× 1)
Phlox douglasii 'Crackerjack' (× 1)
Aubrieta 'Joy' (× 1)
Euphorbia myrsinites (× 1)
Lewisia tweedyi (× 2)
Erinus alpinus (× 1)
Dianthus 'Little Jock' (× 1)

11 Rhodohypoxis baurii (× 10)
12 Armeria juniperifolia (× 1)
13 Pulsatilla vulgaris (× 1)
14 Androsace carnea subsp. laggeri (× 1)
15 Achillea clavennae (× 1)
16 Gentiana septemfida (× 1)
17 Convolvulus althaeoides (× 1)
18 Sisyrinchium subsp. bellum (× 1)
19 Hypericum olympicum 'Citrinum' (× 1)
20 Campanula carpatica (× 1)
21 Aster alpinus (× 1)
22 Geranium cinereum subsp. subcaulescens (× 1)
23 Dianthus 'Annabel' (× 1)
24 Polygala chamaebuxus var. grandiflora (× 1)
25 Erodium corsicum (× 3)

Care and Maintenance

• Weed rock gardens regularly; once weeds have taken hold, they can be difficult to remove.
• The topdressing of gravel will gradually mix into the soil, replace as necessary.

• Cover any plants that may suffer from winter cold with a sheet of glass or a frame covered with polyethylene but allow air to circulate at the sides.
• Water alpines during dry spells.
• Trim back straggling plants.

46

ONE WAY TO DEAL with small corners is to fill them with containers of plants, but while this is useful in paved areas, there is far less work—particularly when watering—if the plants are put into a properly prepared bed. Often awkwardly shaped, corner beds need to be treated with particular imagination. They will then play their part in the whole garden picture.

A gravel finish

Gravel is a very useful garden material. It is a mulch, complements many plants and presents an orderly finish. It can make a highlight of a corner planting as with this 12 × 12 ft (3.5 × 3.5 m) plot. Alternatively, use paving slabs and plant between them, creating a tapestry of cover. Erigeron, acaena, thyme and mint are useful; the last two are aromatic.

Care and Maintenance
- *If planting close to a wall, avoid using tall plants that may bend forward, drawn the light and pushed by winds.*
- *Make sure the gravel is well distributed around the plants and that any small rock are securely bedded in the ground.*

left Waterside planting
can include an exuberant
mixture of foliage and
flowering plants, presenting
luxuriant displays. Here,
white lilies shine out against
clumps of spreading foliage.

below Candelabra primulas
are extremely good plants
for wet and boggy areas.
Both their color and shape
create interest and are seen
at their best against still,
bright water.

special borders

give the garden a distinctive and often unusual

character. From enlivening dry and shaded sites

to enlivening a pond display, these borders often

include plants and materials that are quite

different from those seen in traditional beds.

right Some wetland plants,
such as this *Iris ensata*, can
be grown in an ordinary
border if a pond is not
available, as long as they
have plenty of moisture-
retaining compost.

below Shady and woodland
areas have a protected,
peaceful quality. Hostas are
ideal for such places.

left Grasses are wonderful plants for the varied form and color of their foliage and for their sheer versatility and hardiness. They are an asset in dry beds.

below Succulent plants, such as this beautiful but spiny agave, will thrive in dry Mediterranean-style growing conditions. Gravel creates a perfect background for drought-tolerant plants, particularly architectural specimens like this that deserve space to be admired.

above A subtle variation in colors is always worth trying. The result can be very cool and satisfying, as in this healthy dry border in shades of green and yellow.

right In areas where rainfall has declined it is essential to change to plants that will grow happily in dry conditions. The diversity of suitable plants, often very dramatic in appearance, confirms that a dry climate does not mean dull gardens.

waterside planting

WATER FEATURES add a special dimension to a garden: a soothing sound as a stream trickles or a pool ripples, lively or leisurely movement and subtle reflections or darts of light; all are irresistible to any gardener. Such features allow and call for a lush planting of fresh colors, both in the flowers and the foliage. The whole environment around a water feature creates a tranquillity that is rarely reproduced elsewhere in the garden.

Tools and Materials

spade	bricks	plants for the ledge (*see below*)
soft builder's sand	pieces of sod	
	topsoil	
PVC or butyl membrane pond liner to size	well-rotted compost	lattice pots for planting in the pond

Planting Scheme

1 *Iris pseudacorus* 'Variegata' (× 1)	**6** *Hosta sieboldiana* var. *elegans* (× 1)	**10** *Nymphaea* 'René Gérard' (× 1)
2 *Iris sibirica* (× 6)	**7** *Hosta tokudama*	**11** *Primula pulverulenta* (× 2)
3 *Ranunculus lingua* (× 5)	f. *flavocircinalis* (× 1)	
4 *Phalaris arundinacea* (× 3)	**8** *Mimulus luteus* (× 3)	**12** *Salix babylonica* (× 1)
5 *Typha latifolia* (× 3)	**9** *Hydrocharis morsus-ranae* (× 3)	

Care and Maintenance

Weeds love lush, moist conditions and ust be removed constantly, otherwise they n overrun a planting scheme, making it ok neglected.

Cut back dead foliage in autumn and p-dress the edging bed with organic matter ch as garden compost or leaf mold.

• Many waterside plants are rampant and need to be removed every two or three years. Replant just a few pieces.
• When maintaining the border, be careful not to puncture the liner.
• Check the condition of the liner regularly, looking for any exposed or damaged areas.

ALTHOUGH MANY of the plants grown beside a pond can also be grown in a border, most particularly enjoy moist soil. Avoid plants that prefer dry conditions—this includes most silver-foliaged plants. Those intended to grow in shallow water at the edge and in the pond should be true aquatic plants.

Creating a waterside border
Dig out the pond to the shape required, including a ledge around the edge; this will carry the waterside border. Slope the ledge outward to encourage the absorption of water from the pool. Cover the whole surface with a layer of soft builder's sand to about 2 in (5 cm) in depth to prevent sharp objects from penetrating the liner.

Lining the pond and border
Stretch the liner across the pond so that it extends well beyond the ledge. Place bricks around the edge to keep it stretched, then fill the pond. The liner will sink, taking up the profile of the hole, dragging the bricks inward. Fill the liner to the edge of the ledge. Ease the material into the contours of the ledge and tuck the liner firmly into the bank so that it is concealed.

Making the border
Build a wall of inverted pieces of sod, forming a bank. Fill the space behind this with a mixture of topsoil and well-rotted compost. Allow the soil to settle, then add more water to the pond so that it soaks into the border. If the soil in the border sinks, top it up.

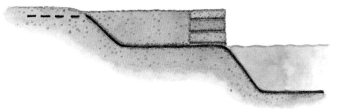

Planting the bed
When planting an edging bed on top of a liner, be very careful not to damage the material when digging. Carefully dig holes and insert the plants. Plant those that require most water, or that will grow with their roots in water, at the edge of the pond. To add variety to the scheme, suitable plants can be placed in the pond itself in special lattice pots. This full scheme is 10 × 20 ft (3 × 6 m).

dry border

GARDENERS THROUGHOUT the world are facing a shortage of water, so it is a good idea to make the most of plants that are used to growing in dry regions. Just as attractive as plants from temperate areas, their more defined growth habits and foliage forms can give a border a striking, architectural appearance. For a neat finish, the ground can be mulched with small stones. These will help preserve moisture and keep down weeds, making the border easy to maintain.

Tools and Materials

spade
tamper or roller
large stones for underlayer
small stones for path
path edging (*optional*)

Planting Scheme

1 *Penstemon heterophyllus* (× 5)
2 *Verbena bonariensis* (× 7)
3 *Sedum telephium* subsp. *maximum* 'Atropurpureum' (× 3)
4 *Euphorbia dulcis* 'Chameleon' (× 3)
5 *Agapanthus* 'Ben Hope' (× 1)

6 *Eryngium giganteum* (× 8)
7 *Pennisetum villosum* (× 1)
8 *Allium hollandicum* 'Purple Sensation' (× 7)
9 *Stachys byzantina* (× 3)
10 *Phormium tenax* (× 1)

11 *Sedum* 'Vera Jameson' (× 3)
12 *Stipa gigantea* (× 1)
13 *Artemisia* 'Powis Castle' (× 1)
14 *Asphodeline lutea* (× 3)
15 *Persicaria affinis* (× 5)
16 *Juniperus scopulorum* Skyrocket' (× 1)

Alternative scheme: succulents

Succulents are ideal for dry conditions, giving a garden a healthy display of lush plants, typified by fleshy leaves. As with the main planting, this irregular bed, which is approximately 18 × 18 ft (5.5 × 5.5 m), is surrounded by an informal gravel path.

Alternative Planting

1 *Cotyledon orbiculata* (× 3)
2 *Dorotheanthus bellidiformis* (× 10)
3 *Jovibarba hirta* (× 10)
4 *Rhodiola rosea* (× 4)
5 *Sedum acre* (× 20)
6 *Sedum aizoon* 'Euphorbioides' (× 8)
7 *Sedum lydium* (× 5)
8 *Sedum spathulifolium* 'Aureum' (× 6)
9 *Sedum spectabile* 'Meteor' (× 3)
10 *Sedum spurium* 'Schorbuser Blut' (× 5)
11 *Sedum telephium* subsp. *maximum* 'Atropurpureum' (× 3)
12 *Sedum* 'Bertram Anderson' (× 6)
13 *Sedum* 'Herbstfreude' (× 5)
14 *Sedum* 'Morchen' (× 3)
15 *Sedum* 'Ruby Glow' (× 3)
16 *Sedum* 'Sunset Cloud' (× 6)
17 *Sedum* 'Vera Jameson' (× 6)
18 *Sempervivum* 'Commander Hay' (× 10)
19 *Sempervivum* 'Glowing Embers' (× 4)
20 *Sempervivum* 'Lady Kelly' (× 5)
21 *Sempervivum tectorum* (× 6)
22 *Yucca flaccida* (× 1)
23 *Yucca gloriosa* 'Variegata' (× 1)
24 *Yucca filamentosa* 'Ivory' (× 1)

are and Maintenance

Be sure that the bed remains well drained. Many dry-loving plants produce decorative d heads that can be kept for autumn interest.

56

THE BEAUTY of drought-tolerant plants is that they need very little attention once established. For the best results, work the empty bed in autumn, adding well-rotted organic material to improve the soil and some sharp sand or fine grit. Together, these additions will help lighten the soil, causing any rain to soak through rapidly.

A suitable path
Paths made of gravelor small stones not only make a good surface on which to walk but also provide a good setting for dry-loving plants.

Making a gravel path
To make a stony path, first remove all weeds and, depending on the size of the path, tamp (right) or roll the surface down for a compact, level finish.

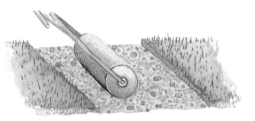

Cover the prepared base with a layer of stones, 1 in (2.5 cm) deep. This should be rolled well into the base (left).

Another method is to dig out the path to a depth of 1–2 in (2.5–5 cm), level it, roll it, and then lay black plastic garden sheeting (right). Bury the edges into the soil on either side of the path.

Finally, for both methods, cover with a loose layer of stones at least 1 in (2.5 cm) deep. Edge the path with wood, stone or bricks (left), or leave the sides vague to merge with the bed.

woodland border

WOODLAND BORDERS conjure up a romantic image of beautiful
flowers in wide, misty glades surrounded by luxuriant trees, an image
well beyond most gardens. However, the idea can be realized on a
much smaller scale with surprising success. Such a border needs only
one or two trees to provide the shade and atmosphere while the
smaller plants create the effect. Indeed, there is no reason why the
whole could not be miniaturized and created under a few large shrubs.

Tools and Materials

spade   sticks
tamper or roller   bark chippings
logs

Planting Scheme

1 *Rosa* 'Ramona' (× 1)
2 *Corylus avellana* (× 1)
3 *Hosta* Tardiana Group
  'Halcyon' (× 1)
4 *Geranium* × *magnificum*
  (× 3)
5 *Dicentra* 'Bountiful' (× 5)
6 *Iris sibirica* (× 1)

7 *Geranium pratense* (× 1)
8 *Alchemilla mollis* (× 2)
9 *Bergenia* 'Silberlicht' (× 3)
10 *Brunnera macrophylla* (× 1)
11 *Campanula latifolia* (× 1)
12 *Digitalis purpurea* (× 5)
13 *Epimedium* × *rubrum* (× 1)

14 *Euphorbia amygdaloides*
  var. *robbiae* (× 3)
15 *Helleborus foetidus* (× 3)
16 *Myosotis sylvatica* (× 3)
17 *Persicaria affinis* (× 3)
18 *Pulmonaria officinalis* (× 3)
19 *Stylophorum diphyllum* (× 2)
20 *Tellima grandiflora* (× 3)

ing underplanting

nhance spring interest, there are many plants that can be added under and
und the main plants. Many of these spring-flowering plants will run to seed,
ning a most desirable carpet of color.

Spring Planting

1 *Anemone nemorosa* (× 4)
2 *Convallaria majalis* (× 4)
3 *Cyclamen coum* (× 8)
4 *Eranthis hyemalis* (× 4)
5 *Galanthus nivalis* (× 20)
6 *Hyacinthoides non-scripta* (× 12)
7 *Narcissus pseudonarcissus* (× 6)

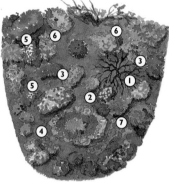

WOODLAND BORDERS extend from under trees where the conditions range from dense to mottled shade. The number of plants that will tolerate full shade is limited, although this is less problematic in spring when the sparser tree canopies allow more light through. For the rest of the year, use the woodland margins to provide color and interest.

Woodland conditions

Trees and shrubs are notoriously hungry and thirsty plants, so the soil should be provided with plenty of well-rotted organic compost. In keeping with a natural setting, this is best provided by leaf mold made by composting any available foliage after it has fallen in autumn. After clearing any weeds, work the proposed border, adding as much leaf mold as possible. This will help the soil to retain moisture but the border will never be as wet as a bed in open ground, so choose plants that will tolerate dryness. Plant in autumn on lighter soils but wait until spring if the soil is at all heavy. This border is 15 × 15 ft (4.5 × 4.5 m).

Creating a bark path

Paths around a woodland border or through shady areas are best kept informal. A natural material for such paths is bark chippings, itself a woodland product. This gives a soft finish and particularly suits meandering paths. To make the path, first compact the soil below the intended path (see page 55).

The sides of a bark path can be left vague to blend into the borders or can be edged with logs to prevent the bark from spreading too far. If logs are used, hold them in place by inserting sticks at intervals on either side.

Pour 2–3 in (5–7.5 cm) of bark chippings along the path. If the layer is deeper than this, the path will be too soft. Rake at regular intervals and top up with fresh bark as the material breaks down into humus.

Woodland bulbs

In spring, before the leaves appear on the trees, woodland areas are often full of bulbs, making the most of the sunlight before leafy canopies darken the ground. Many spring bulbs are suitable for woodland use. The best way to achieve a random planting is to broadcast the bulbs onto the ground and plant them where they fall. The depth of planting varies, but as a rule of thumb always plant three times the depth of the bulb. Snowdrops should be planted while they are "in the green," that is, while they are still in growth, just after flowering and while their leaves are green.

mediterranean border

IN AREAS WHERE HOT, DRY summers are the norm, there is little point in trying to create a lush herbaceous border that prefers cooler conditions. A Mediterranean border is the ideal solution, with plants that are colorful in both their flowers and foliage. Hardy plants, they will succeed in cooler regions where a rather exotic look is desired.

Tools and Materials

spade

tamper or roller

large stones for underlayer

small stones for path

Planting Scheme

1 *Veronica* 'Shirley Blue' (× 6)

2 *Cistus* × *skanbergii* (× 1)

3 *Chamaecyparis lawsoniana* 'Denbury Blue' (× 1)

4 *Althaea officinalis* 'Romney Marsh' (× 3)

5 *Onopordum acanthium* (× 3)

6 *Euphorbia characias* (× 1)

7 *Cistus* 'Anne Palmer' (× 2)

8 *Nectaroscordum siculum* (× 25)

9 *Allium unifolium* (× 25)

10 *Lavandula officinalis* (× 1)

11 *Sedum* 'Herbstfreude' (× 3)

12 *Stachys byzantina* (× 10)

13 *Ballota pseudodictamnus* (× 3)

14 *Salvia* × *superba* 'Superba' (× 2)

15 *Lychnis coronaria* (× 1)

16 *Salvia jurisicii* (× 1)

17 *Acaena saccaticupula* 'Blue Haze' (× 12)

18 *Salvia officinalis* Purpurascens Group (× 2)

19 *Linaria purpurea* 'Springside White' (× 1)

20 *Papaver somniferum* (× 5)

A dry stream bed

In dry areas the garden can be enhanced by taking elements of the Mediterranean landscape and incorporating them into the border. For example, the impression of a dry stream bed can be created through the center of the border.

Dry Stream Planting

Miscanthus sinensis (× 1)
Cordyline australis (× 1)
Agapanthus 'Bressingham Blue' (× 1)
Ophiopogon planiscapus 'Nigrescens' (× 6)
Euphorbia characias subsp. *wulfenii* (× 1)
Eryngium giganteum (× 3)
Callistemon citrinus (× 1)

Dry stream planting
The most appropriate scheme is a sparse planting of grasses and drought-tolerant plants with a jumble of pebbles, smooth rocks, water-worn wood, and old tree stumps lining a shallow gully.

Collecting seeds
Many of the plants in this bed produce seeds. When ripe, the seedpods turn brown or black and the seeds fall away freely when lightly moved. Tip the seeds (or seed head) into a labeled paper bag. Place in a warm airy place where the contents of the bag can dry, but not in a hot place and especially not in sunlight. When dry, sift the seeds to remove detritus, then empty them into a labeled envelope. This can be kept in the refrigerator until required.

64

THE MEDITERRANEAN BORDER has diversity and warmth of color yet presents quite a different quality from the plants most familiar to temperate climates. They are resilient against dry heat and a surprising degree of cold and make few demands, excellent for low-maintenance gardening.

Creating a Mediterranean border

Prepare the bed first then lay the path. Work the plot in autumn, removing any perennial weeds and adding well-rotted organic material. Mediterranean plants like ground that does not remain too wet, so if the soil is heavy clay, add sharp sand or fine gravel to help with drainage. In spring turn over the soil and break it down with a rake, removing any weeds that have appeared over winter. The most suitable pathing is gravel, which can be left to blend with the edges of the bed (see page 55 for construction).This curved site is around 10 × 15 ft (3 × 4.5 m).

Care and Maintenance
• *Trim back plants after flowering.*
• *Some of the seed heads such as the* Allium *and the* Onopordum *make good dried flowers and can be kept in the border or picked for indoor use.*

63

shady border

MANY GARDENS HAVE a shady corner, perhaps in the shadow of an overhanging tree or adjacent walls or fences. In some cases the shade may be dense, in others there may be light from above but the area is never reached by direct sunlight. This situation is one of the most difficult to deal with in gardening terms since most flowering plants need sunshine to do well. However, by rising to the challenge, there are ways of using these areas to advantage.

Planting Scheme

1 *Hosta* Tardiana Group 'Halcyon' (× 1)

2 *Hosta fortunei* var. *aureomarginata* (× 1)

3 *Euphorbia characias* subsp. *wulfenii* (× 1)

4 *Nectaroscordum siculum* (× 10)

5 *Nepeta racemosa* (× 3)

6 *Tanacetum parthenium* (× 6)

7 *Lilium martagon* (× 1)

8 *Smyrnium perfoliatum* (× 5)

9 *Tellima grandiflora* (× 3)

10 *Geranium nodosum* (× 1)

11 *Lamium galeobdolon* (× 3)

12 *Hemerocallis* 'Pink Damask' (× 1)

13 *Dryopteris filix-mas* (× 1)

14 *Carex pendula* (× 1)

15 *Foeniculum vulgare* (× 1)

16 *Hyacinthoides non-scripta* (× 10)

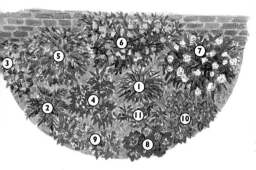

Planting a north wall

Not all gardens can be south- or west-facing, and one of the worst situations in gardening terms is a north wall. This suffers from prolonged or constant shade and, as a result, a marked chilliness when compared to other parts of the same garden. Such an unfavorable microclimate can still support plant life that will cheer a dull corner.

Full-shade Planting

Carex pendula (× 1)
Dryopteris filix-mas (× 1)
Cyclamen hederifolium (× 5)
Euphorbia amygdaloides
var. *robbiae* (× 3)
Garrya elliptica (× 1)
Rosa 'New Dawn' (× 1)
Camellia japonica (× 1)
Alchemilla mollis (× 1)
Geranium macrorrhizum (× 3)
Epimedium × versicolor
'Sulphureum' (× 3)
Hyacinthoides hispanica (× 4)

SHADE USUALLY WORKS hand in hand with other problems. Walls, trees and similar objects not only cast a sun shadow but a rain shadow; this means that the border is deprived of moisture as well as light. An area between two buildings or structures might also be a drafty location since whirling currents of air can be created along alleyways even on apparently windless days.

Overcoming problems
The right choice of plants will minimize the problem of lack of sunlight, and the moisture content of the soil can be improved by the addition of well-rotted organic material (see page 59) and a mulch. Strong winds can be moderated by using resilient shrubs or a built screen as windbreaks. Where part of a border does get the sun, add sun-loving plants; here, in this 6 × 12 ft (1.8 × 3.5 m) bed, nepeta is included.

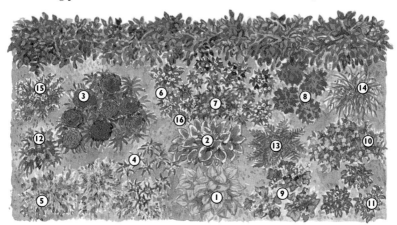

Other Plants for Shade

Anemone nemorosa	Lilium martagon
Arum italicum	Meconopsis betonicifolia
Aruncus dioicus	Omphalodes cappadocica
Astilbe	Omphalodes verna
Cardiocrinum giganteum	Oxalis acetosella
Convallaria majalis	Pachysandra terminalis
Cornus canadensis	Polygonatum × hybridum
Corydalis flexuosa	Primula
Cyclamen coum	Smilacina racemosa
Eranthis hyemalis	Trillium
Euphorbia amygdaloides	Vancouveria chrysantha
Galanthus nivalis	Vinca minor
Helleborus orientalis	Viola odorata
Houttuynia cordata	
Iris foetidissima	
Kirengeshoma palmata	(See also *Woodland Border*,
Lathyrus vernus	pages 58–60)

An ivy corner
A simple but imaginative idea is to fill the shady area with ivy, not in the style of a neglected garden but as a living sculpture. Add surfaces and contours to the space with mounds of earth, tree stumps, or even objects such as old metal chairs, then plant the ivy at 18-in (45-cm) intervals and allow it to ramble freely. The vigorous nature of the plant will come into its own.

rose bed

Roses ARE STILL among the most popular of garden plants. Not only do they provide the garden with masses of beautiful flowers but they also frequently fill it with the most delightful fragrance. Roses are very versatile—they can be used as ground cover, grown as low, medium, or tall bushes, trained around pillars or obelisks, or allowed to scale trellises and even trees. They can be combined with other plants or used by themselves to create a unique feature, the rose garden.

Planting Scheme

1 *Rosa* 'Pink Grootendorst' (× 1)
2 *Salvia greggii* (× 5)
3 *Geranium palmatum* (× 5)

Alternative Modern Shrub Roses

Charles Austin (*apricot and yellow*)   Heritage (*pink*)
Constance Spry (*pink*)   L. D. Braithwaite (*crimson*)
Cottage Rose (*pink*)   Mary Rose (*pink*)
Dark Lady (*deep red*)   Othello (*crimson*)
English Garden (*yellow*)   The Countryman (*pink*)
Gertrude Jekyll (*pink*)   Warwick Castle (*pink*)
Glamis Castle (*white*)   Wife of Bath (*pink*)
Golden Celebration (*yellow*)   Winchester Cathedral (*white*)
Graham Thomas (*yellow*)

Alternative scheme: an obelisk

Rose beds can consist of just shrub roses or they can include low climbers trained up an obelisk or pillar. More vigorous varieties will swamp a pergola or a long trellis (see page 93). The use of attractive garden structures such as these can enhance the impact of the plants.

Alternative Planting

1 *Rosa* 'Alister Stella Gray' (× 1)
2 *Rosa* Graham Thomas (× 4)
3 *Tropaeolum majus* 'Alaska' (× 8)

Care and Maintenance

- *To get the best results from roses, prune regularly.*
- *Be on your guard against diseases, such as black spot, rose rust, and powdery mildew, and pests, such as aphids.*

Charles Austin **Cottage Rose** **Heritage**

Winchester Cathedral **Golden Celebration** **Constance Spry**

A ROSE IS SUCH an impressive, complete plant that a bed using a single variety can work very well; if the plant is large then even a single specimen can make a great impact. Here, the large rugosa rose 'Pink Grootendorst' creates a centerpiece around which a small selection of perennials is arranged. These are planted tight against the rose so they merge to form a bold mound.

Choosing roses

There are literally thousands of roses to choose from and probably the best way to make a choice is to visit a specialist nursery while they are in flower. Various factors influence a gardener's selection: Flower color and fragrance, whether the plant is repeat-flowering, and the ultimate size of the variety are four key elements. For a relatively confined space, as with this 8-ft (2.4-m) bed, size is a significant point.

Planting roses

Prepare the soil and plant. Bare-rooted roses should be planted between autumn and early spring. This is also the best time for planting container-grown plants, although they can be planted any time if kept watered.

Plant associations

Some gardeners like to see bare earth under their roses. However, for an abundant look, there are many plants that work well with roses, including alliums, diascias, anthemises, fragarias, geraniums, persicarias, pulmonarias, stachys and violas. The best place for these companion plants is around the borders where they can both be seen and benefit from the sun.

walk-through
borders are highly sensuous

because they allow the viewer to get among the
plants. This creates a greater intimacy with their
sight, feel, and smell. Where arches or pergolas
are involved, the viewer is totally surrounded by
plants and their fragrance. All gardeners should
allow time to walk through their borders.

above This very romantic
formal paved is promenade
lined with borders and
contained behind box
hedges. The whole is framed
by a series of arches covered
in abundant roses and
clematis. It makes a
wonderful, cool walkway.

right Wide paths created
from irregular-sized paving
slabs run between square
and rectangular beds. The
shapes are formal but the
planting, by contrast, is
exuberant, asymmetrical,
and filled with life.

above A walled garden filled with a profusion
of old-fashioned cottage garden plants. The
narrow path just allows visitors to wander
through the flowers, brushing and smelling
as they go. The discreet path adds to the
sense that this is a secret garden.

74

above Beautiful formality is enhanced by the simplicity of this design. Identical beds spread onto a grass pathway with a central stream gully. The stone edging directs the eye clearly along the straight line while the purple and green add a lively quality.

below The silky heads of this grass, *Hordeum jubatum*, just ask to be caressed as you walk along the central path. They contrast nicely with the cleome beyond, in a more orderly part of the garden.

above A bend in a path adds a note of mystery to any garden scene. Here, a stretch of grass curves away, suggesting a great garden beyond.

below Paths within a path: Here, bold stepping-stones lead in opposite directions while the main grass track forges ahead. Each possibility demands exploration.

edible border

MOST OF THE PRODUCE for the kitchen comes from the vegetable and herb gardens, but there is plenty that can be grown in the more ornamental parts of the garden. Many flowers can be eaten or used as a garnish for food, and many vegetables are so decorative that they more than earn their place in borders. Creating a border with culinary as well as decorative value can be very enjoyable and provides great economy of space in a small garden.

Planting Scheme

1 *Atriplex hortensis* 'Rubra'
(red mountain spinach: *edible young leaves*) (× 60)
2 *Calendula officinalis*
(pot marigold: *edible flowers*) (× 30)
3 *Cynara cardunculus*
(cardoon: *edible blanched stems*) (× 6)
4 *Helianthus annuus*
(sunflower: *edible seed*) (× 20)
5 *Hemerocallis*
(daylily: *edible opening buds*) (× 8)

Pergola planting

A pergola, whether a substantial wooden structure or a more refined metal frame, should complement the pathway borders in shape and plantings.

Using a pergola

A pergola straddling the path allows the addition of several types of vegetables or fruit. The overall effect is that of an avenue of produce through which a shady walk can be taken. For a temporary display, green beans, climbing French beans, or squash and zucchini can be grown. For a more permanent display, grapes (above right), apples, or pears can be trained over the arches, or a combination of the two (above left). Keep the climbers well trained and pruned to get the best from them and also to allow more light to reach the plants in the borders.

Care and Maintenance

• *When you are harvesting only parts of plants, take from a different plant each time so that there is time for regrowth and to avoid creating an unbalanced appearance in the bed.*

78

ALTHOUGH THE MAJOR concern of this border is decorative, many of the elements are made up from edible plants. Tradition tends to dictate that vegetable and flower gardens are kept separate, but there is no real reason to do so. The unexpected presence of decorative vegetables can give freshness to a planting. The soil preparation, planting, and maintenance for an edible border are just the same as for any other.

Edible ornamentals
All the edible plants in this border will enhance a salad while the opening buds of the daylily can be chopped up and stir fried. These beds are 6 × 20 ft (1.8 × 6 m) but limited space provides even more reason to include edibles.

Warning
Not all garden plants are edible and only those known to be safe should be eaten or used as food decoration.

Edible flowering plants and vegetables
The list of plants that are edible in whole or part is very long. Here are some of the most rewarding, both in terms of their decorative qualities and for culinary purposes. The less familiar edible parts of some popular vegetables are pointed out.

Vegetables
carrots (foliage)
Swiss chard (foliage)
tomatoes (fruit)
peas (flowers and fruit)
corn (foliage)
lettuce (bronze foliage)

Flowering plants
Mentha (mint: leaves)
Viola odorata (sweet violets: flowers)
Tropaeolum majus (nasturtium: flowers)
Thymus (thyme: leaves)
Borago officinalis (borage: flowers)
Rosa (roses: petals)
Rosmarinus officinalis (rosemary: flowers, leaves)

cottage garden path

THE WEALTH OF PLANTS in a traditional cottage garden creates a wild, romantic air. A riot of colors and shapes speaks of the informality of a typical country border, which can be created in any garden if the whole scheme is sympathetic to a freely planted approach. For those who like an unpredictable display, this is the perfect path-side look.

Planting Scheme

Year-round interest
1 *Juniperus communis* 'Depressa Aurea' (× 1)

Spring flowering
2 *Erysimum* (× 7)
3 *Forsythia* (× 1)
4 *Narcissus* (× 19)
5 *Primula vulgaris* (× 8)
6 *Tulipa* (× 16)
7 *Viola × wittrockiana* (× 5)

Summer flowering
8 *Achillea ptarmica* The Pearl Group (× 3)
9 *Alcea rosea* (× 8)
10 *Alchemilla mollis* (× 6)
11 *Dianthus* 'Mrs Sinkins' (× 6)
12 *Digitalis purpurea* (× 5)
13 *Echinops ritro* (× 3)
14 *Erigeron* 'Serenity' (× 3)
15 *Erodium manescaui* (× 1)
16 *Geranium himalayense* (× 3)
17 *Hemerocallis fulva* (× 3)
18 *Lavandula angustifolia* (× 1)
19 *Lychnis coronaria* (× 3)

20 *Lysimachia punctata* (× 3)
21 *Lysimachia nummularia* 'Aurea' (× 3)
22 *Oenothera biennis* (× 6)
23 *Papaver somniferum* (× 6)
24 *Phlox* 'Cherry Pink' (× 6)
25 *Rosa rugosa* (× 1)
26 *Stachys byzantina* (× 3)
27 *Trollius europaeus* (× 1)
28 *Viola cornuta* (× 3)

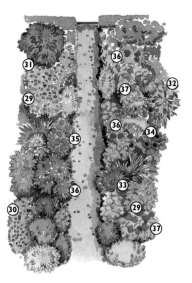

Maturing time

These pathway borders are 13 × 30 ft (4 × 9 m) and will begin to mature in two years, although the shrubs will take many years to reach their ultimate size.

Late-summer and autumn interest

The cottage garden should provide interest throughout the year. Although many plants in this border flower for a short period, their foliage is long-lived. Some plants flower repeatedly over a long period or bloom again in autumn.

Late-season Planting

29 *Anemone* × *hybrida* (× 4)
30 *Aster novae-angliae* 'Andenken an Alma Pötschke' (× 5)
31 *Aster novi-belgii* (× 3)
32 *Buddleja davidii* (× 1)

33 *Crocosmia masoniorum* (× 6)
34 *Helianthus annuus* (× 5)
35 *Sedum spectabile* (× 3)
36 *Solidago* 'Cloth of Gold' (× 4)
37 *Tanacetum vulgare* (× 3)

Alternative pathways

As with all garden styles, the appearance of the path can alter the impression made by the cottage garden.

Bricks

A simple pattern in the brickwork and attractive weathering suit the country style.

Stepping-stones

Stones bedded in beaten earth lead the eye along the path.

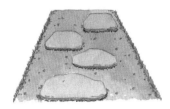

Grass

Introduce patterns by setting the lawn mower at different heights.

THE CHARM OF THE ORIGINAL Victorian cottage gardens lay in the fact that they were simply a wonderful collection of plants. With little knowledge of the niceties of garden design, cottage gardeners freely filled gaps in a border and allowed annuals to seed unhindered, creating a busy picture of fruit, vegetables, and native ornamentals.

Planning a cottage garden

When laying out a cottage garden, a sense of freedom should be maintained. For an authentic touch, only traditional plants (pre-c.1900) should be used, although the spirit of a cottage garden will allow any colorful plants to be included providing they do not need too much pampering. Fruit and vegetables should also be included if possible.

Practicalities

Besides the useful presence of edible plants, cottage gardens exhibited other practical characteristics. Tight planting prevented weeds from growing, and the use of a wide range of robust plants helped to prevent any one pest or disease from causing wholesale damage.

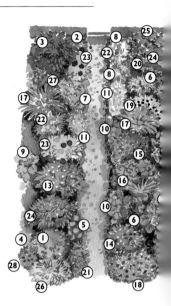

Care and Maintenance

• *Make sure that any tall or flopping plants are well supported. It will be difficult to reach them once the border is in full growth.*

• *While abundant growth can be very attractive, make sure that paths are not made dangerous by trailing stems.*

81

scented path

BORDERS THAT LINE PATHS are always welcome because they bring the viewer close to the plants. This is doubly rewarding with fragrant borders since the sense of smell as well as that of sight is stimulated; in many cases, the action of rubbing against the plants as you pass releases the fragrance. Lavender and rosemary have very distinctive aromas that pervade the air for a long distance, far beyond the pathway.

Alternative Scented Plants

Fragrant Foliage	Fragrant Flowers	
Lavandula	Berberis	Lupinus
Aloysia triphylla	Choisya ternata	Matthiola
Artemisia	Convallaria majalis	Nicotiana
Mentha	Daphne	Osmanthus
Monarda didyma	Dianthus	Philadelphus
Myrtus communis	Erysimum	Reseda odorata
Origanum	Hesperis matronalis	Rhododendron (azaleas)
Rosmarinus	Hyacinthus	Rosa
Salvia officinalis	Iris unguicularis	Sarcococca
	Lathyrus odoratus	Syringa
	Lilium	Viburnum
		Viola odorata

Alternative scheme

Cottage-style gardens have paths over which everything seems to spill. Paths for this kind of border should be wide enough to accommodate both the spreading plants and the passage of people. Typical fragrant plants for this type of display are the border pinks, especially the old-fashioned varieties.

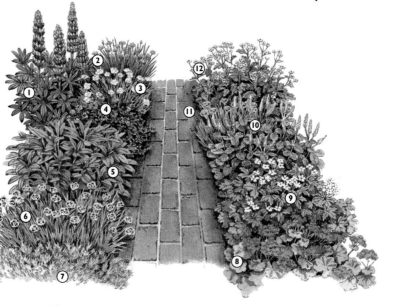

Alternative Planting

1 *Lupinus* 'Kayleigh Ann Savage' (× 1)
2 chives (× 3)
3 *Dianthus* 'Haytor White' (× 1)
4 thyme (× 1)
5 sage (× 1)
6 *Dianthus* 'Gran's Favourite' (× 2)
7 *Artemisia caucasica* (× 1)
8 *Alchemilla mollis* (× 2)
9 *Geranium sanguineum* 'Album' (× 1)
10 mint (× 1)
11 *Dianthus* 'Laced Monarch' (× 1)
12 *Tanacetum parthenium* 'Aureum' (× 1)

86

FRAGRANT PLANTS SHOULD be used more frequently in the garden as they add another special dimension to it. Although some odorous plants are positively offensive, there are many that produce the most wonderful perfumes, such as lavender. These are perfect for creating a relaxing atmosphere, the raison d'être of many a garden today. This delightful path is 9 × 25 ft (2.5 × 7.5 m).

Design

It is important that a path is sufficiently wide for its purpose. Most garden paths should be wide enough for two people to walk side by side; an allowance of at least 5 ft (1.5 m) should be made. Paths that are purely for access can be narrower but should still take a wheelbarrow comfortably.

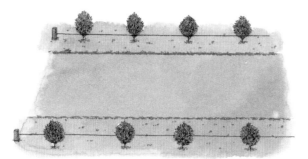

Preparing and planting the beds

Using a string line as a guide, plant the lavenders in a straight row, each being close enough to the next to merge with it when in full growth, which is about 2 ft (60 cm) all around. To make a consistent picture, use the same colored variety for all the plants. Seed-grown plants might be cheaper, but the colors can vary. Plant the shrubs to the same depth as they were in their pots, firm down, and water. If possible, mulch the plants to retain moisture and inhibit weeds.

Care and Maintenance

• *Lavender should be pruned in late summer. Remove all flower stems and cut away about 1 in (2.5 cm) of the previous season's growth. Shape the beds into a slightly undulating low hedge (above).*

courtyard path

IN SMALL PAVED GARDENS there seems to be little choice but to grow plants in pots. However, for a larger display, a generous raised bed is ideal since it holds sufficient soil to sustain a number of plants, both permanent perennials and seasonal annuals. As well as permitting more versatile planting schemes, raised beds create different levels, which add interest to the space. If they border a path, the extra height can be used to display angular and trailing foliage.

Tools and Materials

spade	bricks, stone, or	pieces of sod or a
trowel	concrete blocks	sheet of horticultural
broken rocks	broken pots or stones	polyethylene
concrete		timbers or railway ties
		(*no foundations needed*)

Planting Scheme

1 *Corylus maxima* 'Purpurea' (× 1)
2 *Phormium tenax* 'Purpureum' (× 4)
3 *Heuchera micrantha* var. *diversifolia*
.'Palace Purple' (× 8)

Planning

A courtyard, with its strong architectural identity, lends itself to symmetrical, well-blended displays and plants with bold foliage forms. So plan raised beds accordingly, using plants that will stand up to close scrutiny as people walk along the path. Full foliage and fragrance are assets. This large raised bed is × 12 ft (2.4 × 3.6 m).

Care and Maintenance
• *Keep the soil in raised beds topped up and check that the structure is draining efficiently.*

way ties
are laid directly onto a flat base. When them, stagger the vertical joins, as with work, to give a firmer finish. Leave small for drainage. Remember to lift the rs with care because they are heavy.

Traditional stone
Slabs of light brown and gray stones give quite a different finish to a wall of bricks. They are particularly well suited to cottages and country houses. If the house is of stone, ideally the same material should be used for the bed.

RAISED BEDS ARE not difficult to create, and once filled with soil they can be treated like any other border, with the full range of plants that implies. They allow great scope for the garden designer, but it is essential to plan and build these structures carefully if they are to fit and work well in a garden.

Materials

A variety of materials can be considered for building a raised bed: brick, as here, stone, concrete blocks, and wood. Wood is probably the easiest to use, especially if old railway ties can be found; these are heavy beams of timber that make sturdy walls. They are longer lasting than other forms of wood because they have been impregnated with tar, but that is also their drawback. In hot conditions they ooze tar.

Foundations

Brick, stone, and concrete blocks are used in the same way. If the bed is not being built on a solid base, dig out a foundation about 10 in (25 cm) deep. A 4-in (10-cm) layer of broken rocks should be packed into this, topped by a 6-in (15-cm) layer of concrete. The wall is built on top of this.

Drainage

It is most important that drainage holes are left in the lower levels of the brickwork to allow excess water to drain away (left). A few gaps in the cement can also be sufficient.

Finishing details

For brick walls, a line of tiles can be added toward the top (right). This detail is not essential but partly decorative and partly to direct water away from the wall so that the surface is not stained by repeated drenchings.

Before planting

To aid drainage, add broken pots or stones to a depth of 3 in (7.5 cm) or more then a layer of upturned pieces of sod (above right) or horticultural polyethylene with drainage holes. Fill with good-quality loam with plenty of well-rotted organic matter and some grit to help drainage. Firm down as you go. Overfill the bed because the soil will sink with time.

rose trellis walk

FOR A GARDEN TO BE SUCCESSFUL it needs to benefit from different heights and contours. A meandering trellis covered in plants makes a beautiful feature that draws the eye above the ground and can lead it to a picturesque detail, perhaps a fountain, bench, or spectacularly planted bed. When the trellis travels the length of a pathway it can also be enjoyed on a leisurely stroll; add the romance and sweet fragrance of roses and you will have made a favorite part of any garden.

Planting Scheme

1 *Rosa* 'American Pillar' (× 3)
2 *Rosa* 'Félicité Perpétue' (× 2)
3 *Geranium* 'Johnson's Blue' (× 32)
4 *Rosa* Constance Spry (× 2)
5 *Rosa* L. D. Braithwaite (× 3)

Alternative Roses

Climbers and Ramblers	**Shrubs**
'Albéric Barbier' (*yellow and white*)	Charles Austin (*apricot and yellow*)
'Alister Stella Gray' (*yellow and white*)	English Garden (*yellow*)
'Blush Noisette' (*pink*)	Gertrude Jekyll (*pink*)
'Cécile Brünner' (*pale pink*)	Glamis Castle (*white*)
'Leverkusen' (*lemon yellow*)	Graham Thomas (*yellow*)
'Maigold' (*yellow*)	Heritage (*pink*)
'Mme Alfred Carrière' (*white*)	Mary Rose (*pink*)
'New Dawn' (*pink*)	Othello (*crimson*)
'Paul's Himalayan Musk' (*pale pink*)	The Countryman (*pink*)
'Paul's Scarlet Climber' (*scarlet*)	Warwick Castle (*pink*)
'Sanders' White Rambler' (*white*)	Winchester Cathedral (*white*)

Alternative trellising

very attractive version can be made by
king the tops of the uprights with a thick
ece of rope. Additional lengths of rope will
ve the roses extra support. Tie in the roses as
ey climb. Look out for and secure any stray
ms to prevent accidents.

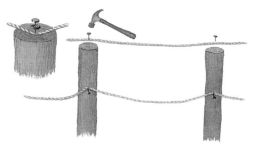

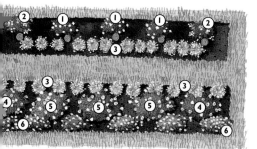

Alternative scheme: a white walkway

The perennial favorite is a white scheme.
For freshness and purity nothing can
match it. If space is limited, white also
has an advantage over stronger colors,
which can dominate a garden scene.
There are scores of beautiful white roses
to choose from.

Alternative Planting

sa 'Mme Alfred Carrière'
3)
sa 'Seagull' (× 2)
anthus 'Mrs Sinkins'
umerous)
sa Winchester Cathedral
2)
sa Glamis Castle (× 3)
anium sanguineum
oum' (numerous)

THE TRELLIS IS A traditional garden structure that continues to have great appeal. Its versatility and ease of use make it an asset in gardens of any size. The simple, open structure of rustic trellising allows light through while giving ample support to climbing plants. Always remember the underplanting to give the trellis an abundant, balanced appearance.

A rose walkway
A trellis running the length of a path is an excellent device. It gives structure to a design, and height across the garden, not just at the edges. For a rose walkway, think of repeat-flowering climbing or rambling varieties; these will give a longer season. There is no reason why the roses should be restricted to one type; each section can be different or two roses can be mixed in one section. If the walk is narrow, 'Zéphirine Drouhin', which is thornless, makes a good choice. This trellis bed is 4×25 ft (1.2×7.5 m).

Erecting a trellis
Make sure the structure is st[r] because it will have to carry [the] weight of the roses and also withstand the impact of wind. The posts must be secure in [the] ground, in holes 2 ft (30 cm) deep, bedded on broken roc[k] and fixed with concrete (ab[ove]). For a solid finish, the top bea[m] and diagonals must fit tightl[y] into generous notches at eac[h] joint (left), strengthened wi[th] nails or screws.

Shrub rose border
To complement the trellis, a border of shrub roses can be planted on the other side of the path. The colors should be harmonious with those on the trellis but the bushes should be lower so that other parts of the garden can be seen from the walk. The whole will create a vista of dense roses.

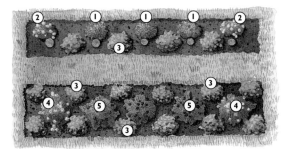

Underplanting
The soil can be left bare under both the trellis and the shrub border, but more interest is created if they are underplanted. This will also help to minimize weeds. Keep the planting simple. Do not choose too many different plants, one variety may well be sufficient. These plants should be a finishing touch —the roses are the chief glory.

basic techniques

SOIL PREPARATION

The most important aspect of creating a border is thorough preparation. Without it, even the best designs are likely to fail after a year or two, smothered by weeds or starved for nutrients and moisture.

It is important to remove all perennial weeds before planting. Even a small piece of root will reemerge as a weed, by which time it might be difficult to remove without digging up the whole border again. With lighter soils it may be possible to dig the soil and remove any weeds at the same time, but with heavier soils it may be necessary to use a weedkiller; if so, always follow the directions on the package. Dig the soil in the autumn and plant in the spring. This will allow any small piece of weed left in the soil to reveal itself so that it can be removed. In areas with warmer winters it is also possible to dig in spring and plant in autumn.

DOUBLE DIGGING

All borders should be worked but they will be better, especially on heavy soils, if they are double-dug so that the lower portion of earth is also broken up. Do not dig if the soil is too wet. When the border is dug, as much well-rotted organic matter should be incorporated into the soil as possible. This not only improves the structure of the soil but provides nutrients for the plants. Its fibrous nature also helps preserve moisture deep in the soil where the plants' roots need it. Consequently, when double-digging it is important to add generous quantities of organic material to the lower level. Once the soil has been worked, leave it for several months. This will allow the rain and frost to break it down and kill any pests. Residual weeds will also reappear. Avoid walking on the area while it is weathering.

Double digging
1 *Dig a trench, 12–18 in (30–45 cm) wide and 12 in (30 cm) deep. Save the removed earth.*

2 *Work the trench for an additional 12 in (30 cm) and add organic matter. Dig out the next trench and use the earth to fill the first.*

3 *As before, work through the layer below, breaking up the ground with a fork and adding organic material.*

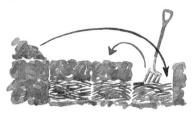

4 *When you have reached the end of the border, fill the final trench with the earth removed from the first trench.*

GARDEN COMPOST

One of the best ways of providing organic material for the garden is to make your own compost. Almost all plant material can be used unless it is too woody or contains weed seeds (woody material can be used once it has been shredded). Avoid diseased material or virulent weeds. Uncooked vegetable waste from the kitchen is recommended.

Place all the material in a container that has air holes in the sides. Avoid creating too thick a layer of any one material, such as grass cuttings. Keep the bin moist but covered so that the compost retains heat and does not get too wet and chilled in rain. Turn the heap occasionally.

If possible, have two bins: one for collecting material and one in use; three is even better, the extra bin decomposing.

PLANNING

When planning a border, or even a whole garden, there are several basic points to consider before you begin to draw up a plan. The first is to assess want you want to achieve. You may, for example, want a low-maintenance border, or a bright, fun border,

or a romantic display in pastel tones; plenty of flowers for cutting might be a priority, or you might prefer a largely foliage effect.

Next, look at where you want to put the border and consider its physical attributes. Does it get plenty of sun or is it in perpetual shade? Is the soil acid or alkaline? Is it wet or dry or just about right? Is it heavy or sandy? All these factors will have a bearing on how much work you will need to put in and on what plants you can and cannot grow. For example, if you live on a chalky soil you will not be able to grow rhododendrons.

After this, decide what plants you want to use to create the desired effect. This is best done over at least one season so that you can go around gardens, notebook in hand, compiling a list of desirable plants. Looking through books also provides plenty of ideas. Having completed your list of plants, it is important to find out whether you can get them locally or if you will have a long search. Adjust your list accordingly.

You are now ready to plot the planting. Using squared paper, draw out the border to scale and then mark out the plants, drawing them at their eventual spread (below). You do not need to be a good draftsman. Adjacent colors should be compatible and the border should have an even spread of interest throughout the year. It is a good idea to draw the bed at different seasons so you can judge the success of the plan and from the front to compare the plants' relative

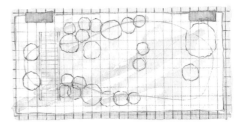

heights. If problems appear through these sketches, it is so much easier to correct them on paper than after planting.

PLANTING

Before planting, rake or lightly turn over the soil, removing any weeds that have appeared. If only a small amount of organic material was added when the soil was being prepared, a light dressing of a general fertilizer can be raked into the surface. Always follow the directions on the package.

Do not plant in extremes of weather, that is, when it is too hot, wet, or cold. The best time for planting shrubs and trees is from late autumn to early spring, and for perennials either autumn or spring. Annuals should not be planted until the threat of frost is passed if they are tender, or in autumn or spring if they are hardy.

Position the plants, still in their pots, on the border to get some visual idea of how the display will look (below). Make any changes you think are necessary. Dig a hole wider than each plant's rootball and insert the plant so that it is at the same depth as it was in its pot or, if it is bare-rooted, in its previous bed. If the roots have become pot-bound or tangled, gently tease them out and spread them in the hole. Fill the hole and firm the soil around the roots.

When planting trees and shrubs, dig a hole much larger than the plant's rootball and work plenty of well-rotted organic material into the bottom of the hole. Also mix some into the soil that will go back into the hole once the plant is in place. If staking the tree or shrub, position the stake before planting so that you will not drive the stake through the roots.

USING A MULCH
Once all the plants are in the bed, water them thoroughly, rake over the surface to level it off, and then apply a mulch. Mulches are an important part of gardening. They cover the surface of the soil, helping keep the moisture in, preventing weed seeds from germinating, preventing the surface of the soil from hardening, which would restrict the entry of air and moisture, and can create an attractive background against which to display the plants.

There are two types of mulches, organic or inorganic. Organic ones consist of chipped bark, leaf mold, spent mushroom compost, or even grass cuttings and straw.

The last two are unattractive but are valuable in areas that cannot be seen, such as the backs of borders. Inorganic mulches include plastic sheeting (which is ugly and should be covered with soil, gravel, or other stones), gravel, or pebbles. Gravel is good for alpine beds and dry borders.

MAINTENANCE
The best borders are those that are well maintained. Issues such as staking, pruning, and watering must be considered.

Twiggy-branch supports
These are versatile, flexible supports that can be drawn together and tied to form a supporting case around vulnerable plants. They can be removed easily.

Netting support
A net support is a permanent device. The plant grows up and through the mesh which, in time, will be hidden by foliage.

String and stakes
Stakes with a network of strings are useful as a temporary support for larger, spreading shrubs until they are established.

STAKING

Always stake plants that could blow over or become top-heavy in rain. There are many ways to stake perennials. Tall flower spikes, such as delphiniums, can be supported by individual canes; clumps can be held by twiggy-branch supports; netting by posts.

Staking trees
A single tie should be placed low down to support a tree. This will give suficient extra stability until the tree is established.

Staking standard bushes
Standards and spindly trees need a taller stake than more robust trees, fitted with two ties (the first tie is shown here, positioned high up the stem).

Commercially produced stakes are also available. Stake the plants when they are half-grown; do not wait until they blow over.

Trees and shrubs should be staked with a single or double stake. For most trees it is sufficient to use a single tie low down, 12 in (30 cm) from the ground. For standards and spindly trees use a taller stake and two ties.

DEADHEADING

As a general rule, always cut off any dead or dying flowers, unless you want to collect the seeds or save the seed heads for decoration. Many perennials, such as nepeta, a number of geraniums, alchemillas and oriental poppies, should be cut to the ground after flowering; this will encourage a fresh crop of leaves to grow, making the plant useful for foliage effect.

WATERING

Water plants in dry conditions, making certain that they get a thorough soaking, the equivalent of at least 1 in (2.5 cm) across the surface. Do not water in full sun. Feeding should not be necessary if the border is top-dressed regularly. Every autumn, fork in the organic mulch and replace it with a layer of farmyard manure or garden compost. In spring, work this into the border and reapply the usual mulch.

WEEDING

Remove any weeds on sight. Regular checks will keep weeds under control; if left, they can become difficult and time-consuming to eradicate. With conscientious application it should be possible to hand-weed a border. Chemical herbicides should be avoided on a planted area.

AUTUMN CARE

In autumn, most perennials should be cut back. This task can be left until spring so that the old stems give the crown some protection from frosts, although tidying during the dormant season means that there is less to do during the spring rush.

PRUNING

Ornamental trees and evergreen shrubs generally do not need pruning.

Removing old, dead, and weak wood
A shrub like the one above should be thoroughly pruned. Dead and weak wood and some of the old stems should go.

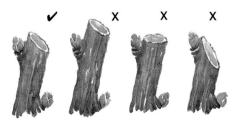

Pruning cuts
Correct pruning cuts are very important to the health of plants. Cuts should be sloping, just above a viable bud (above, far left).

But remove any dead or dying branches, and stems can be removed for aesthetic reasons. By contrast, most deciduous shrubs benefit from regular attention. The aim is to keep the bush healthy and vigorous so that it produces good foliage and flowers. To do this, up to one-third of the old wood should be cut off each year, encouraging new growth. As a general rule, the best time to prune is immediately after the bush has finished flowering. Diseased, dead, or weak growth should also be removed. Pruning cuts should be sloping, just above a viable bud.

SOWING SEED
There are two ways of sowing seeds: directly in the soil and into trays or pots.

3 Pour some water into the drill. This will help to consolidate the furrow and will ensure that the seeds receive adequate moisture.

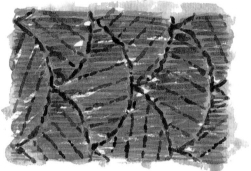

Direct sowing: annuals
If clumps of plants are required, mark out the ground with fine sand before sowing.

4 Sow the seeds, sprinkling a fine line into the shallow trench. Do not overfill as overcrowding can starve seedlings of nourishment.

Direct sowing: perennials
1 Dig the soil well, then rake it over to produce a fine tilth for sowing.

5 Draw the soil back into the drill with the back of the rake and lightly water.

DIRECT SOWING
If sowing annuals into a border, break down the dug soil into a fine tilth with a rake. If several clumps of plants are required, mark out each area with some sand so that it is easy to see where to sow. Scatter the seeds over the required area; gently rake them in. Water with a fine-spray watering can. If sowing perennials in a seed bed, draw out a shallow furrow with the edge of a hoe using a guide line if necessary, dampen it, and scatter a sprinkling of seeds along it. Draw the soil back into the drill, then water.

2 Make a shallow drill, or furrow, with the edge of a hoe, using guide lines if necessary. Guides can be made using pegs and a length of string.

POT SOWING

If only a few plants are required or if it is necessary to sow the seeds in gentle heat, they should be sown in a tray or pot. Using a good seed compost, fill the pot and tap it to settle the contents; level and lightly press the compost down. Sow the seeds thinly and cover with a layer of fine grit or compost. Water the compost carefully. Many annuals need to be placed in a warm environment such as a propagator or heated greenhouse.

Planting bulbs
As a general guide, make sure the planting hole for a bulb is at least three times as deep as the bulb is tall.

Sowing in a pot
Once the seeds have been sprinkled in a pot, cover with compost or a fine grit as recommended for the particular plant.

Planting in a tray
Once seedlings have grown in a tray, they should be pricked out carefully and planted on in individual pots to continue growing.

Perennials rarely require heat and can be kept outside in a sheltered position. Keep moist until the seeds germinate and then prick out into trays or individual pots. Tender seedlings that have been sheltered should be hardened off in a cold frame before being planted after the threat of frost has passed.

BULBS

Spring-flowering bulbs are planted in autumn; summer- and autumn-flowering bulbs are planted in spring. As a rule, the depth of the planting hole should be at least three times the height of the bulb. While daffodils, tulips, and several other bulbs can

be purchased as dry specimens, it is better to buy many others either "in the green", that is, freshly dug with their leaves still green, or growing in pots. For example, snowdrops should always be purchased in the green, but cyclamens are best bought as potted specimens. Some plants can be relied upon to increase of their own accord. These are often naturalized bulbs, which have been left to grow in grass or under trees. If they become congested, dig them up and replant.

BUYING PLANTS

There are several ways of acquiring plants for a border. The simplest is to buy them. Garden centers sell a reasonably wide range, but specialist nurseries have a much larger selection, including unusual plants. Many nurseries also send plants by mail order, which is a great advantage if they are far from your home. Order early, as demand can outstrip supply for many catalogue plant. Inform the nursery if you expect to be away when the order is sent, otherwise you might come home to a box of dead plants. When buying plants, do not always go for the largest specimen. A medium-sized plant, free from pests and diseases, is best. Do not buy pot-bound plants (below).

The alternative to buying plants is to grow them from seeds, by division, or from cuttings. This is a much cheaper approach, but plants will need time to mature. Rare plants are often available only as seeds.

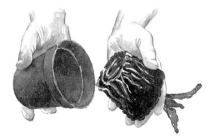

useful addresses

Rice Creek Gardens
1315 66 Avenue NE
Minneapolis, MN
55432

Sandy Marsh Herb
Nursery
316 Surrett Cover Road
Leicester, NC
2848

John Scheepers
23 Tulip Drive
Bantam, CT
06750

Shady Oaks Nursery
112 Tenth Avenue SE
Waseca, MN
56093

Shepherd's Garden
Seeds
7389 West Zayante Road
Felton, CA
95016

Smith Nursery Co.
P.O. Box 515
Charles City, IA
50616

Stokes Seeds Inc.
Box 548
Buffalo, NY
14240

Thomesville Nurseries
P.O. Box 7
Thomesville, GA
31792

Thompson & Morgan
P.O. Box 1308
Jackson, NJ
08527

Van Engelen Inc.
Stillbrook Farm
Maple Street, 307-B
Litchfield, CT
06759

André Viette Farm
& Nursery
Route 1, Box 16,
Fishersville, VA
22939

Wavecrest Nursery and
Landscaping Co.
2509 Lakeshore Drive
Fennville, MI
49804

Wayside Gardens
Highway 254
P.O. Box 1
Hodges, SC
29695-0001

White Flower Farm
30 Irene Street
Torrington, CT
06790

Woodlanders Inc.
1128 Colleton Avenue
Aiken, SC
29801

Canada

Alberta Nurseries & Seeds
P.O. Box 20
Bowden
Alberta
Canada
T0M 0K0

C.A. Cruikshank Inc
1015 Mount Pleasant
Road
Toronto
Ontario
Canada
M4P 2M1

Woodland Nurseries
2151 Camilla Road
Mississauga
Ontario
Canada
L5A 2KI

**PLANTERS AND GARDEN
STRUCTURES**

Bamboo Fences
179 Boylston Street
Boston, MA
02130

Brooklyn Botanic Garden
1000 Washington Avenue
Brooklyn, NY
11225

Colonial Garden
Products
P.O. Box 371008
El Paso, TX
79937

Country Casual
17317 Germantown Road
Germantown, MD
20874

Gardener's Eden
P.O. Box 7307
San Francisco, CA
94120-9600

Gardeners Supply Co.
126 Intervale Road
Burlington, VT
05401

Joan Cook
P.O. Box 21628
Fort Lauderdale, FL
38335

Kinsman Company
River Road
Dept. 625
Point Pleasant, PA
18950

Smith and Hawken
2 Arbor Lane
P.O. Box 6900
Florence, KY
41022-6900

Treillage
420 S. 75th Street
New York, NY
10021

**LUMBER AND BUILDING
SUPPLIES**

Home Depot
Check your local
telephone directory for
your nearest store.

Lehigh Portland
Cement
718 Hamilton Mail
Allentown, PA
18105

index

credits

The publishers would like to thank the following illustrators for their contributions to the book: Elizabeth Pepperell, Martine Collings, Tracy Fennell, Valerie Hill, Stephen Hird, Sarah Kensington, Amanda Patton, Lizzie Sanders, Helen Smythe, and Ann Winterbotham.

They would also like to thank the owners of the following gardens for their help: Axletree Garden and Nursery, Peasmarsh, East Sussex; Bates Green, Arlington, East Sussex; Beth Chatto Gardens, Elmstead Market, Essex; Hailsham Grange, Hailsham, East Sussex; King John's Lodge, Etchingham, East Sussex; Merriments Garden, Hurst Green, East Sussex; Queen Anne's, Goudhurst, Kent; Rogers Rough, Kilndown, Kent; Upper Mill Cottage, Lodse, Kent; Hadspen Garden and Nursery, Castle Cary, Somerset; Cinque Cottage, Ticehurst, East Sussex; Sticky Wicket Garden, Buckland Newton, Dorset; Snape Cottage, Chaffeymoor, Dorset; Grace Barrand Design Centre, Nutfield, Surrey; Holkham Hall Garden Centre, Holkham, Norfolk; Wyland Wood, Robertsbridge, East Sussex; Long Barn, Kent; and Hatfield House, Hertfordshire.

The photographs in this book were taken by Stephen Robson except for the following which are courtesy of Jerry Harpur: (t = top, b = bottom, c = center, l = left, r = right) p.34 tr, bl, cr, br; p.35 br; p.74 tl; p.75 tl, tr, br; p.104; p.111

acknowledgements

The author would like to thank all those involved in bringing this book into the light of day: Anne Ryland who made the book possible by commissioning it; Lynn Bryan for editorial work during the early stages; and Sarah Polden who took over and shaped the book into its final form, as well as giving plenty of encouragement; Stephen Robson, who manipulated the camera so adroitly; Mark Latter for the hours he spent on the design and his endless stream of faxes; and all the illustrators for the delightful artworks.

Thanks also to all the owners of the beautiful gardens who allowed us to photograph them especially for this book.